Contents

Where is Belfast? 4

The story of Belfast 6

Belfast today...8

The sea and the hills 10

Belfast and the *Titanic* 12

The Waterfront 14

The zoo and castles 16

Museums, theatres and galleries..........18

Hidden gems...20

Shopping in Belfast................................22

Sport in Belfast 24

Festivals and celebrations 26

Map of Belfast city centre.....................28

Glossary 29

Find out more 30

Places to visit..31

Index...32

Some words are shown in bold, **like this**.
You can find out what they mean by looking
in the glossary.

Where is Belfast?

Every country has a capital city. The capital is the most important city in a country. Belfast is the capital of Northern Ireland. The Northern Ireland **Assembly** is in Belfast. It makes some of Northern Ireland's laws.

Around 334,000 people live in Belfast.

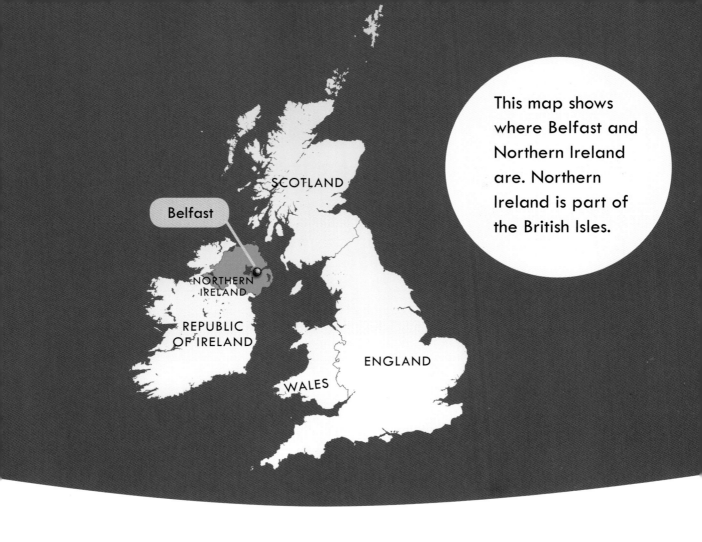

This map shows where Belfast and Northern Ireland are. Northern Ireland is part of the British Isles.

Belfast is the biggest city in Northern Ireland. It is on the east coast of Northern Ireland. Belfast is partly in **County** Antrim. It is also partly in County Down.

The story of Belfast

About 400 years ago, Belfast was a small village on the banks of the River Lagan. The river now flows through tunnels under the high street. **Docks** were built where ships could load and unload wool and **grain**.

For many years, shipbuilding was Belfast's biggest industry.

People have painted pictures on this wall in Belfast. They celebrate the end of The Troubles.

Between 1968 and 1998, there was dangerous fighting in Northern Ireland. Some people wanted Northern Ireland to be part of the Republic of Ireland. Others wanted it to be part of the United Kingdom. This time was known as The Troubles.

Belfast today

Today, Belfast is a busy city. People visit to eat and drink in the many restaurants and coffee shops. There are also many shops to go to. Street musicians play traditional Irish music.

Shoppers can enjoy live music in Belfast city centre.

St Anne's Cathedral has a stainless-steel **spire**. It was added in 2007.

In Belfast's city centre, there are many parks and areas to sit or walk in. There are also old buildings, such as St Anne's Cathedral. It is lit up at night.

The sea and the hills

Belfast sits at the end of Belfast **Lough**. The Lough is a finger-shaped stretch of water that pokes inland from the Irish Sea. The Lough links Belfast to the sea.

Belfast Lough is 5 kilometres (3 miles) across from one side to the other.

Cave Hill Country Park is a popular place for a walk.

There are hills all around Belfast. They are only a short distance from the city centre. You can climb up Cave Hill, near Belfast Castle, for great views across the city.

Belfast and the *Titanic*

The famous ocean liner named the *Titanic* was built in Belfast. It sank in 1912 when it hit an iceberg. Over 1,500 passengers lost their lives. The story of the *Titanic* is now told at the Titanic Belfast Visitor Centre.

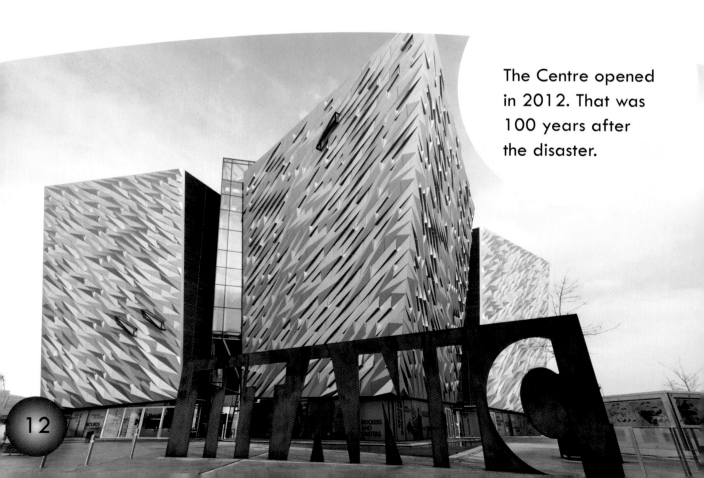

The Centre opened in 2012. That was 100 years after the disaster.

A ceremony is held at the Titanic Memorial every year.

The Titanic **Memorial** stands near Belfast City Hall. It was put up in 1920 to remember 22 local people who died when the *Titanic* sank. It stands in the Titanic Memorial Gardens.

The Waterfront

There is a bridge over the River Lagan as well as **pedestrian** walkways. The area along the river is called the Waterfront. There are concerts and open-air events at Custom House Square. There is an ice rink at Christmas time.

The Custom House stands on the Waterfront.

The Salmon of Knowledge is 10 metres (33 feet) long. It is covered with **ceramic** tiles.

Look out for a giant model of a fish called the Salmon of Knowledge. Its nickname is the Big Fish. Salmon lived in the river but it became polluted. People cleaned out the river and the salmon returned. The model was made to celebrate.

The zoo and castles

Belfast Zoo was built on a hill in the north of Belfast. Over 1,000 animals live there. These include Asian elephants, giraffes and lemurs. The zoo is helping to **breed** animals that are endangered in the wild.

Lemurs wander around the grounds at Belfast Zoo.

These are the Parliament buildings near Stormont Castle.

Belfast has two castles. Belfast Castle is in Cave Hill Country Park. It was built in 1865, and has lots of turrets and towers. Stormont Castle is close to the **Parliament** buildings. It is home to the Northern Ireland **Assembly.**

17

Museums, theatres and galleries

The Ulster Museum is in Belfast's Botanic Gardens. The museum has history, art and nature zones. It has displays from Northern Ireland and around the world. The museum is packed with treasures, including Viking jewellery and dinosaur bones.

A Stegosaur skeleton is one of many exhibits in the Ulster Museum.

The Grand Opera House opened in 1895.

Belfast has many theatres and art galleries. The Metropolitan Arts Centre (called the MAC) shows art from all over the world. The Grand Opera House stands in the city centre. You can go there to see plays, musicals and pantomimes.

Hidden gems

Belfast has interesting places that visitors might miss. Look for the Alice Clock at the Fountain Centre. Every three hours, Bible characters go round it. On the other hours, characters from *Alice in Wonderland* go round.

The Alice Clock is the only **animated** clock in Ireland.

Artist Deborah Brown designed *Sheep on the Road.*

There are lots of sculptures to spot on Belfast's streets. Look out for flying figures on the Ulster Bank building. There is also a flock of sheep outside the Waterfront Hall!

Shopping in Belfast

You can buy almost anything at St George's Market. There are fresh eels, local meat and creamy Irish cheese. You can also get tasty Irish bread there, such as soda bread or potato bread.

There are lots of fruit and vegetable stalls at St George's Market.

A huge glass dome keeps the rain out at Victoria Square.

Wellington Street is one of Belfast's most popular streets for shopping. It has fashion shops, jewellery shops, gift shops and cafés. Victoria Square is a big shopping centre. It has four floors of shops under a huge glass roof.

Sport in Belfast

Gaelic football and **hurling** are traditional Irish sports. You can watch them both at Casement Park stadium in Belfast. More than 30,000 fans cheer their favourite teams there.

In hurling, players hit the ball with a flat stick.

There are many paintings of George Best on Belfast's streets.

The famous footballer George Best (1945–2005) was born in Belfast. He played for Northern Ireland and Manchester United. He is a local hero. The George Best Belfast City Airport is named after him.

Festivals and celebrations

The *August Féile* (meaning August Festival in Irish) is held every year in West Belfast. There is a huge carnival parade. Another popular event, the Festival of Fools, takes place in May every year. It has comedy shows and acrobats.

Street performers entertain crowds at the Festival of Fools.

There are always lots of shamrocks to be seen on St Patrick's Day!

On 17 March, Irish people celebrate St Patrick's Day. St Patrick is the **patron saint** of Ireland. In Belfast, there is a grand parade. People often dress up in green clothes and wave **shamrock** flags.

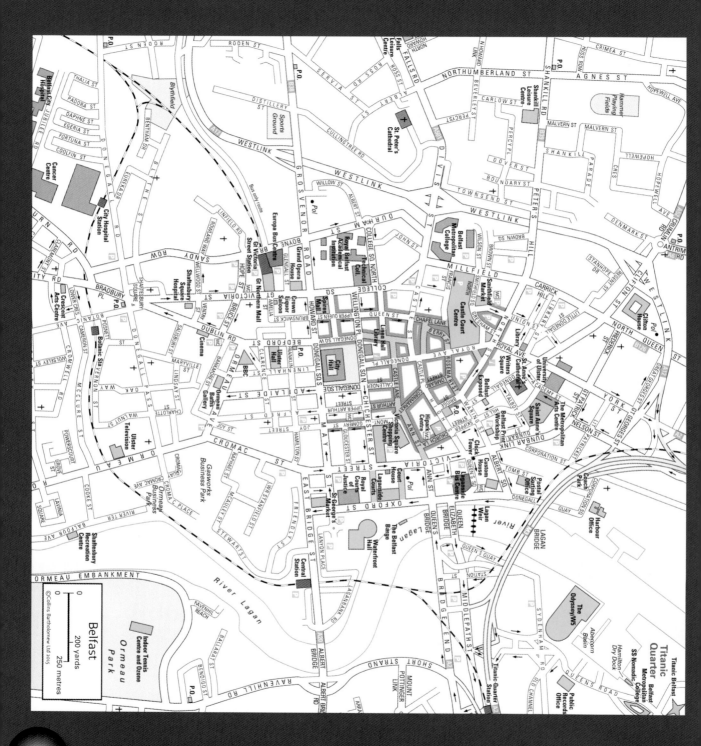

28

Glossary

animated made to move so that it looks alive

assembly group of people who make some of the laws for their country

breed when animals have babies

ceramic made of clay that has been

county geographical area within a country

dock place where ships are built or where they are loaded and unloaded

grain fruits or seeds of plants, such as wheat and maize, used to make flour and other foods

hurling popular sport that is similar to hockey

lough (say 'lock') Irish word for a lake

memorial statue or sculpture that reminds us of a person or event

Parliament place where a country's laws are made

patron saint saint who is thought to protect the people of a country

pedestrian person who is walking

shamrock plant that looks similar to clover

spire upright structure on top of a church tower or other building

Find out more

Books

Great Breaks: Belfast (Insight Guides, 2014)

Let's Visit Northern Ireland, Annabelle Lynch (Franklin Watts, 2015)

The Story of the Titanic for Children, Joe Fullman (Carlton Kids, 2015)

Websites

www.familyadventureproject.org/2012/05/top-10-ideas-for-family-craic-fun-in-belfast
Ideas for fun things children can do on a visit to Belfast.

www.titanicfacts.net/building-the-titanic.html
This Titanic Facts website has lots of facts about building the *Titanic* in Belfast.

visit-belfast.com
This is the official website for visitors to Belfast, with lots of information on sights to see, places to eat and events.

Places to visit

Places mentioned in the book
Belfast Zoo, Antrim Road, Belfast BT36 7PN
www.belfastzoo.co.uk

Titanic **Belfast**, Olympic Way, Titanic Quarter, Belfast BT3 9EP. This is the world's largest *Titanic* exhibition.
www.titanicbelfast.com

Ulster Museum, Botanic Gardens, Belfast BT9 5AB
nmni.com/um

More places to visit
Belfast Community Circus, 23–25 Gordon Street, Belfast BT1 2LG
www.belfastcircus.org

Botanic Gardens, College Park, Botanic Avenue, Belfast BT7 1LP
www.visit-belfast.com/things-to-do/member/botanic-gardens

Ulster Folk and Transport Museum, Cultra, Holywood, Belfast BT18 0EU
nmni.com/uftm

Index

Alice Clock 20
art galleries 19
Assembly 4, 17
August Féile 26

Belfast Castle 11, 17
Belfast Lough 10
Belfast Zoo 16
Best, George 25
Botanic Gardens 18

Cave Hill 11, 17
City Hall 13
Custom House Square 14

Festival of Fools 26
festivals 26–27
Fountain Centre 20

Gaelic football 24
Grand Opera House 19

map of Belfast city centre 28

Northern Ireland 4, 5, 7, 17,
   18, 25

population 4

Republic of Ireland 5, 7
restaurants 8
rivers 6, 14, 15

Salmon of Knowledge, the 15
Sheep on the Road 21
ships 6
shopping 8, 22–23
sport 24–25
St Anne's Cathedral 9
St George's Market 22
Stormont Castle 17
St Patrick's Day 27

theatre 19
Titanic 12, 13
Titanic Memorial 13
Titanic, Visitor Centre 12
Troubles, The 7

Ulster Bank building 21
Ulster Museum 18

walkways 14
Waterfront Hall 21
Waterfront, the 14–15